The Basics

Zach Windahl

Introduction

My name is Zach Windahl and I created Sunday School: The Basics because it is my goal in life to make it easier for you to understand the Bible and to grow in your relationship with God.

A little bit about me first: In 2014, I hit a low spot in my life. Like low low. Everything that I touched began to fail. I had never felt so lost. If you know me, you know I always have a plan. But this time I didn't. I was at the bottom. Broken and lost. I had spent the last several years focusing on myself and trying to become the best person I could be. But, to tell you the truth, I'm weak when I try to live life on my own. From the outside, everything looked great but the inside was a whole different story.

I started to contemplate what all of this was about. I grew up considering myself a Christian, but I had no idea what that truly meant. I hadn't been following God's call at all. I still believed in Him, I just wasn't pursuing Him. I hadn't been to church in over a year for the simple fact that I couldn't stand the majority of Christians that I met because I didn't trust them. They all seemed so fake. Little did I know that the darkness inside of me at the time didn't like the Light inside of them.

So I sat there thinking..."Is life really all about going to college, getting a job, getting married, having kids, buying new things, and then (hopefully) one day retiring so I can enjoy life?"

Really? That's it?
That all seemed so shallow to me.

Then, I looked at religion. Nearly every religion outside of Christianity takes their faith so seriously, it's insane. And then there's us. Where only 45% of Christians read the Bible once a month and the fact that a ton of "Christian" ideals are pretty skewed from the Bible itself. I was fed up. So I read the Bible. Front to back. In 90 days.

I was blown away by how different the Bible actually is, compared to how it's presented in America. But that's what makes us Christians, right? The fact that we believe and follow Jesus?

Nothing was lining up. I was confused.

So I went on my own "Search for Meaning" journey. I quit my job and moved to a little beach town on the Sunshine Coast of Australia to study the Bible for twelve hours per day, six days a week. That's a pretty big leap if you ask me. And at 27 years old it may not have been the wisest of decisions, but I wouldn't have changed it for anything.

My whole reason for this journey was to build a firm foundation in my faith - one that could not be crumbled by society. And that's exactly what I got, plus more.

And that's what my hope is for you. That you are able to build a firm foundation in your faith through resources like Sunday School: The Basics. Especially in a time when growing in your relationship with God is the most important thing that you can do.

How it works

THIS BOOK IS ABOUT THE BASICS.

The basics which build the foundation on which your faith should be based. Whether you recently accepted Jesus as your Savior or are just curious about Christianity in general, this book is for you.

SUNDAY SCHOOL: THE BASICS IS SPLIT INTO SEVEN MAIN SECTIONS:

God the Father and what it means to be a child of God.

Jesus Christ and how he saved you and me.

The Holy Spirit and the power we are given.

The Bible and the story of humanity as a whole.

Prayer and how we communicate with God.

Grace and the favor that is placed upon us.

Community and the importance of doing life with others.

I couldn't be more excited for what God is going to do in you and through you this season as you grow closer to Him. I love you. I believe in you. Let's go!

-Z

God the Father

ALSO KNOWN AS:

Lord God, YHWH, Abba, Elohim, Jehovah, Ancient of Days,
Most High, El-Shaddai, Adonai

WHO IS GOD THE FATHER?

First things first. In order to understand who God is, you need to understand that He consists of three equal persons: God the Father, God the Son and God the Holy Spirit. This is called the "trinity". There is nothing else in our reality that we can compare it to, which makes understanding the three-part nature of God fairly difficult. Many theologians have tried to break it down into analogies, such as water, ice, and mist or all of the pieces of an egg: shell, yolk, and egg white. All of which have their own purpose separately as well as their own purpose together. Our God, the one True God is three-in-one.

The initial person of the trinity is God the Father. We see God the Father predominantly in the first section of the Bible, called the Old Testament, where we begin to understand the nature of God. We see Him as holy, faithful, just, all-knowing, and a protector, as well as, a friend, loving, a provider, and as a true father figure to His children, pouring out unconditional love on them.

WHAT DOES THAT MEAN FOR ME?

God the Father loves His Son, Jesus, more than anything in the world. Since we have accepted Jesus into our lives and we are now viewed through the lens of Jesus (which we will look at next), God the Father loves us the exact same way, as one of His own children. So we are called "children of God". This is the best news ever. No matter what your relationship with your earthly father is, God calls you His child and wants to love you even better.

Not only is God now our eternal Father figure, but all sorts of blessings come along with that. We are now loved, provided for, and protected. Scripture says that we are co-heirs (Romans 8:17), new creations (2 Corinthians 5:17), and holy priests (1 Peter 2:5). There is nothing we can do to run away from the love of the Father. It's eternal and unconditional. You just have to accept it.

QUESTIONS

How is your relationship with your earthly father?

How does that influence your view of God the Father?

How does learning about His love make you feel?

_____

_____

_____

_____

_____

_____

_____

_____

_____

_____

_____

_____

_____

_____

_____

_____

_____

_____

Jesus Christ

WHO IS JESUS CHRIST?

The second person of the trinity is God the Son, Jesus Christ. In order to understand the importance of Jesus, you need to have a big picture understanding of the whole story.

In the beginning, God created two people: Adam and Eve. Most of the earth was consumed by evil at the time, aside for one area called the Garden of Eden, where Adam and Eve were told to cultivate. In the Garden they had a perfect relationship with God. One day a serpent came on the scene and convinced them to go against God's plan (God always gives us a choice to either obey His word or not)...Adam and Eve sinned. In Christianity, this timeframe is called the "Fall of Man" and that one decision changed the course of humanity because it now put a barrier between Man and God. As a response, God said that one day He would create a Son through Eve that would crush the serpent's head and the serpent would bite his heel. This may be confusing but stick with me.

Fast forward and at the beginning of the Bible we meet a gentleman named Abraham. God said that through Abraham was going to be the birth of a new nation, God's chosen people. One of Abraham's sons was named Judah and God promised that the Savior would come through the line of Judah. A while later, God explains things even more and says that the Savior will be from the line of King David. At this time in history, God's presence resided in the temple (for the most part) and very few people could have a personal relationship with God, like before the Fall of Man.

In the second section of the Bible, called the New Testament, we are introduced to a man named Jesus. This is the Messiah, the Savior, the Chosen One that the people have been waiting for since the beginning of time. Jesus was there to redeem humanity. He was 100% man and 100% God.

Jesus was born of a virgin, lived a sinless life and was crucified for the sins of mankind. The shedding of His sinless blood was necessary in order to pay for all of our sins. So now, if we accept Jesus into our heart, when God the Father looks at you and me, He sees His Son Jesus, spotless and redeemed. Jesus then rose from the dead on the third day and ascended to the right hand of the Father in Heaven, who will one day return again for his "Bride", the Church, and will restore earth to its original intent forever.

WHAT DOES THAT MEAN FOR ME?

This is incredible news for us because by believing in Jesus alone and turning from our sins we are saved from God's wrath and given eternal life. We no longer have to perform for God to bless us, He just loves us as-is.

QUESTIONS

Have you asked Jesus into your heart to be your Savior and Lord?

What else do you know about Jesus?

Do you think Jesus is accurately portrayed in the media?

_____

_____

_____

_____

_____

_____

_____

_____

_____

_____

_____

_____

_____

_____

_____

_____

_____

THE
BIBLE
IS
GOOD
FOR
YOU

The Holy Spirit

WHO IS THE HOLY SPIRIT?

The third person of the trinity is the Holy Spirit, God's presence on earth. We first see the Holy Spirit hovering over the chaos at the beginning of the Bible before anything or anyone was created. Then we begin to see the Spirit come upon different people throughout the Old Testament, enabling them to do great and wondrous things. In the New Testament, when Jesus was baptized, the Holy Spirit descended from Heaven and rested upon him in the form of a dove. The Spirit remained with Jesus for the rest of his life, which allowed him to produce good "fruit" and perform miracles, such as healing the sick, prophesying, and raising people from the dead.

When Jesus left the earth, the Spirit descended upon all of his disciples, empowering them to also perform miracles and lead others to Jesus. The Spirit is still present today, alive and active, moving in ways that our minds can't even comprehend.

WHAT DOES THAT MEAN FOR ME?

Just as the Holy Spirit descended upon the disciples back then, he descends upon those of us who believe today and empowers us to do things we can't do on our own. He is our helper, teacher, guide to truth, and encourages us to share our faith. He gives us spiritual gifts, produces godly characteristics within, and even uses us in supernatural ways to share his love with others. The more time you spend in God's presence, the more He will use you in incredible ways.

QUESTIONS

Did you have any knowledge of the Holy Spirit before? What was it?

Have you been filled with the Holy Spirit?

How can you tell that the Holy Spirit is working in your life?

_____

_____

_____

_____

_____

_____

_____

_____

_____

_____

_____

_____

_____

_____

_____

_____

The Bible

ALSO KNOWN AS:

The Word, Word of God, Holy Book, Scripture, Canon, Sword, the Good Book

WHAT IS THE BIBLE?

To put it simply, the Bible is God's Word. It tells the story of God's love for humanity. The Bible is accurate, authoritative, inspired by the Holy Spirit and applicable to our everyday lives.

The layout of the Bible is a collection of 66 books, split into two sections called the Old Testament and the New Testament. The Old Testament contains 39 books that tell about the history of God's chosen people, "Israel", and the struggles that they went through when choosing to do life with and without God's help. The New Testament contains 27 books that describe the life of Jesus and the early church. Even though there are two major sections of the Bible, the overarching theme of the story is God's desire for humanity to know Him, love Him, and trust Him. The Bible ends by telling us about a day in the future when Jesus will return and restore everything.

WHY SHOULD I STUDY THE BIBLE?

The Bible is the most important book you could ever read and study. The more time you spend in it, the more God will speak to you through His Word. Its purpose is to teach, correct, and develop you into the person that God made you to be. It answers questions, brings clarity, teaches us about God, and shows us that He has a plan for us. The key will be to not get overwhelmed by such a big book. It may not make sense at first, but keep diving in and your life will be changed for the better.

QUESTIONS

What are your thoughts on the Bible?

What role do you think the Bible should play in your life?

How can you incorporate studying the Bible into your everyday life?

_____

_____

_____

_____

_____

_____

_____

_____

_____

_____

_____

_____

_____

_____

_____

_____

_____

Prayer

WHAT IS PRAYER?

Prayer is conversation with God. To put it as simple as possible, prayer is when you talk to God. And you can tell him everything. He isn't afraid of your thoughts or your situation. Since He is already all-knowing, nothing will shock Him. Nothing is too big or too small to pray about because God wants to be involved in every single part of your life. You can ask for help, guidance, clarity, wisdom, or just share about how grateful you are. Prayer doesn't have to be long and drawn out either. It can be short and sweet if you'd like it to be. All God wants is for you to talk to Him with an open heart and be transparent with your thoughts and feelings.

WHY SHOULD I PRAY?

Not only is the ability to pray a miracle in itself because you are able to talk directly to the God of the Universe, BUT prayer changes your life in many other ways too.

Prayer gives us strength.
Prayer leads to breakthrough.
Prayer makes us more like Jesus.
It builds our relationship with God.
It provides restoration.
It brings forgiveness.
And God speaks back to us when we speak to Him.

QUESTIONS

Have you ever prayed before?

Do you think prayer is important?

How can you incorporate prayer into your life more?

_____

_____

_____

_____

_____

_____

_____

_____

_____

_____

_____

_____

_____

_____

_____

_____

_____

_____

_____

Grace

ALSO KNOWN AS:

Favor, Acceptance, Purpose, Kindness, Blessing, Compassion, Mercy

WHAT IS GRACE?

Grace is the unmerited favor of God upon our lives. It's what saves us. There is nothing we can do to gain God's grace, it's all a free gift from Him.

WHY IS GRACE IMPORTANT?

In order to understand God's grace, you need to go back to before you accepted Jesus into your heart. Back then you were a sinner, guilty of breaking God's laws, deserving of death. The only way to redeem your soul was through Jesus.

Enter: Grace.

When we trust in Jesus to save us, God by His grace forgives us of our sins and transforms us into new creations completely...the old is gone, the new has come. Grace also equips us to walk out the plans God has for our lives. We don't deserve it, but God gives it to us anyway because He loves us unconditionally.

QUESTIONS

How has your life changed since you accepted Jesus into your heart?

Why do you think God chooses to give us grace even when we don't deserve it?

Have you ever witnessed God's favor on your life?

_____

_____

_____

_____

_____

_____

_____

_____

_____

_____

_____

_____

_____

_____

_____

_____

_____

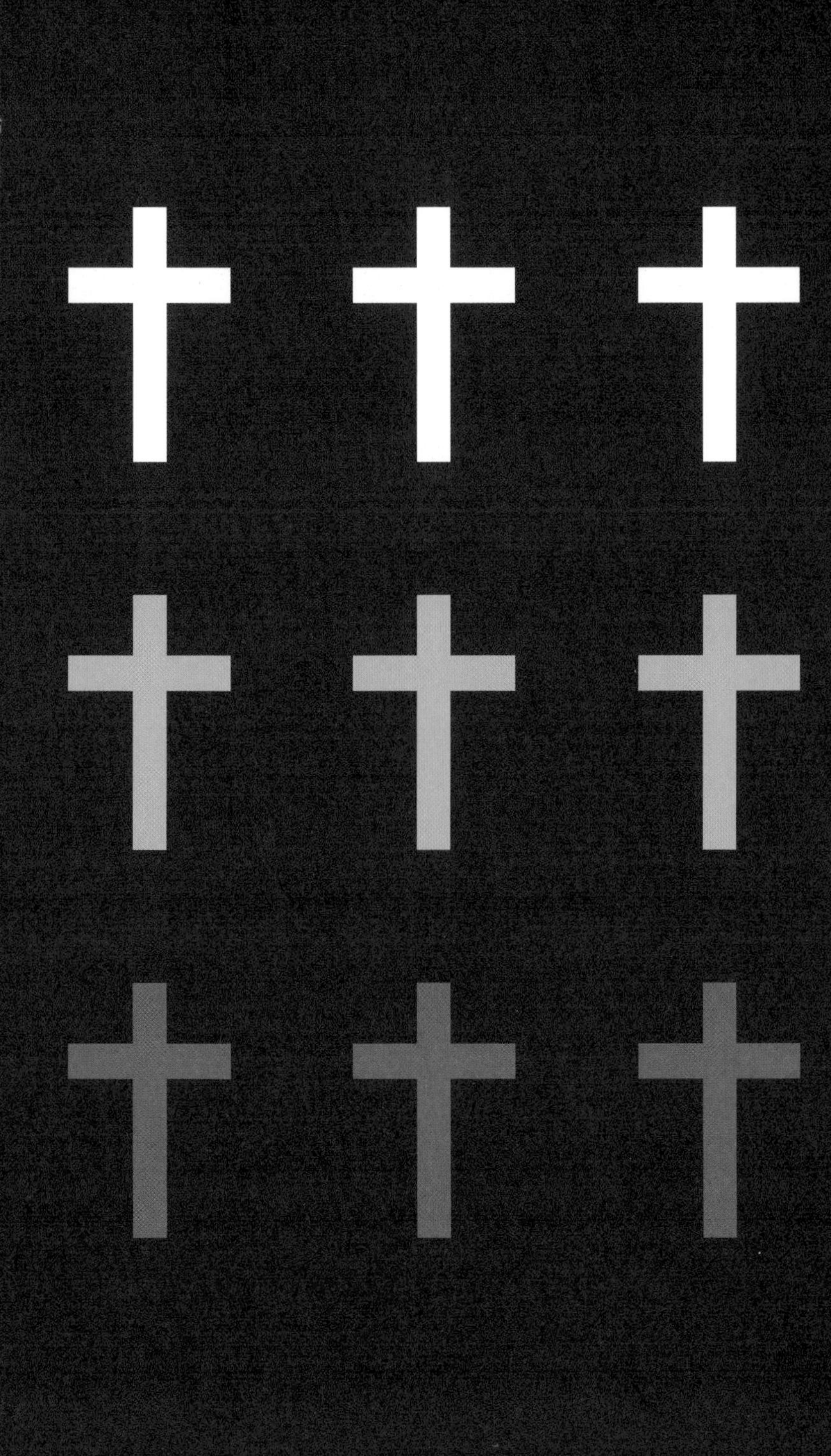

Community

WHAT IS COMMUNITY?

Christian community is special. There's nothing like it when it's done well. Christian community refers to a group of people that have been united through faith in Jesus. It's the church, whether big or small. Community functions to support people in their faith journey and to grow together. It's a safe place for people to be taught, encouraged, and corrected in their faith.

WHY SHOULD I BE PART OF A CHURCH COMMUNITY?

Every Christian should be part of a church community because the Christian faith was not meant to be done alone. Life is meant to be done with others. And getting plugged into a solid Christian community will only push you further along in your relationship with God. A healthy community will help you when you are down, build you up, be a shoulder to cry on, celebrate alongside you, and answer your questions about God.

Once you pick a church community in your area that you want to be a part of, there are multiple ways that you can get involved. You can serve on a team, attend a small group, take a next steps class, or just begin by having meals with other people in the community. If you don't know where to begin, ask a staff member of the church and they can help point you in the right direction.

QUESTIONS

Are you plugged into a solid church community yet?

If not, is there a church community in your area that you want to be a part of?

In what ways do you want to get plugged into a church? (ex. serving, small groups, next steps class, etc)

_____

_____

_____

_____

_____

_____

_____

_____

_____

_____

_____

_____

_____

_____

_____

_____

SUNDAY.

BEST DAY OF THE WEEK

Salvation

By now you should have a good understanding of the basics and what it means to walk out a Christian lifestyle. If you have not already done so, the next step on your faith journey is to begin a personal relationship with God whereby you will be saved from the consequences of your sins. This is called salvation.

As Christians, we are saved by grace through faith in Jesus Christ. Jesus died and rose again just to pay the price for our sins. Salvation doesn't come from our good deeds or by doing anything special, it's a free gift from God just because He loves us so much. We need to turn away from of our sins, believe that Jesus Christ is God's Son and our Savior, and submit to Him as Lord of our lives. By doing so, we receive salvation and eternal life. How awesome is that!

If this is something you want for your life, repeat this prayer:

"Jesus, I believe that you are the Son of God and Savior of the world. I believe that you died for my sins and rose from the dead. I believe that through your sacrifice, I am a new person. Forgive me for my sin and fill me with your Spirit. Today, I choose to follow you for the rest of my life as Lord of my life. Amen."

NEXT STEPS

- Tell another Christian that you accepted Jesus into your life.

- Find a local church community to get plugged into.

- Try to read the Bible and spend time in prayer for at least 10-15 minutes every day.

- Get baptized.

SUNDAY.

At Sunday, we know that you want to grow in your relationship with God. In order to do that, you need to understand the Bible better. The problem is that seems like such a big task, which can be overwhelming. We think it should be easier, so we simplify things for you.

Here's how it works:
1. We create resources.
2. You use the resources.
3. You grow in your faith.

If you want to learn more about the Bible, but aren't sure where to begin, our other product *The Bible Study: A One Year Study of the Bible that Focuses on How Each Book Relates to You* is a great place to build your foundation. To pick up your copy of *The Bible Study* today, please visit *www.thebrandsunday.com*, so you can stop feeling overwhelmed and start being confident in your relationship with God.

About the Author

ZACH WINDAHL

Zach Windahl has helped thousands of people understand the Bible better and grow closer to God. He runs the brand Sunday and is the author of several books including The Bible Study, The Best Season Planner, and the Sunday Journal. He lives in Miami, Florida.